ちょびっツ
Chobits

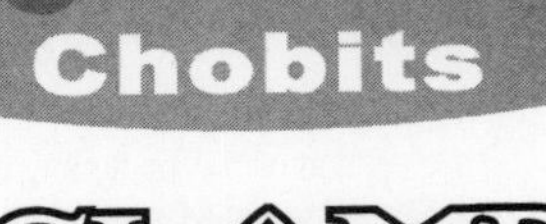

Satsuki Igarashi
Nanase Ohkawa
Mick Nekoi
Mokona Apapa

Translator - Shirley Kubo
English Adaption - Jake Forbes
Retouch & Lettering - Kyle Plummer
Cover Layout - Anna Kernbaum

Senior Editor - Jake Forbes
Managing Editor - Jill Freshney
Production Coordinator - Antonio DePietro
Production Manager - Jennifer Miller
Art Director - Matthew Alford
Director of Editorial - Jeremy Ross
VP of Production & Manufacturing - Ron Klamert
President & C.O.O. - John Parker
Publisher - Stuart Levy

Email: editor@TOKYOPOP.com
Come visit us online at www.TOKYOPOP.com

A TOKYOPOP® Manga
TOKYOPOP® is an imprint of Mixx Entertainment, Inc.
5900 Wilshire Blvd. Suite 2000, Los Angeles, CA 90036

ISBN: 1-59182-005-7

First TOKYOPOP® printing: July 2002

10 9 8 7 6

Printed in the USA

CHIRP
CHIRP
URGHH...
はたっ
I FEEL SICK...
WHAAA?!
ころん

ちょびっツ

Chobits

◂chapter.13▸

HUNHH?
CHI?
IS IT MORNING ALREADY?

THAT'S RIGHT! MS. SHIMIZU DROPPED BY LAST NIGHT OUT OF THE BLUE.
だらだら
SWEATING IT
ムニャムニャ
RUB
YAAAWN... WHAT TIME IS IT?
SHE ASKED IF SHE COULD STAY OVER AND WE ENDED UP DRINKING 'TIL DAWN.
YAWN
MAN, WE GOT HAM- MERED!
THEN I... I... I TOTALLY BLACKED OUT! WHAT HAPPENED NEXT?!
DON'T WORRY, HIDEKI. I DIDN'T TAKE ADVANTAGE OF YOU.
WHA- WHA- WHAT DO YOU MEAN, TAKE ADVATAGE?

I DIDN'T DEFLOWER YOU.
WHAT!?
WHA?
WHOA!
WAIT!
CALL ME ROMANTIC, BUT I THINK YOUR FIRST TIME SHOULD BE WITH SOMEONE YOU LOVE.
YOU GOT DRUNK AND STARTED TAKING YOUR CLOTHES OFF.
DOH!
T-TOOK MY CLOTHES OFF? HOW FAR...?
SMILE
YOU WERE AVERAGE-SIZED.
YOU SAW MY--?!
NO WAY!
WHAT!

AVERAGE-SIZED.
HIDEKI IS AVERAGE-SIZED.
CHI! YOU DON'T HAVE TO REMEMBER THAT!
OH MY GOD!
CHI?
WE'D BETTER GET GOING. IT'S ALMOST TIME FOR CLASS...
BETTER GO CLEAN UP.
WAIT A MINUTE... HOW DOES MS. SHIMIZU KNOW THAT I'M STILL A VIRGIN?
LIFT
WHERE ARE MY CLOTHES?
I GUESS ALL THAT BOOZE MADE ME TALKATIVE.

I'D LEND YOU A TOOTH-BRUSH, BUT I DON'T HAVE AN EXTRA.
THAT'S ALRIGHT.
I BROUGHT MY OWN SINCE I WAS PLANNING ON STAYING OUT ALL NIGHT.
GRAB
YOU MADE PLANS TO STAY WITH ME?!
NOT EXACTLY.
THEN WHY DID YOU COME HERE?
MAYBE BECAUSE I'M A COWARD...
I DON'T KNOW.
MS. SHIMIZU...

MUCH BETTER!
I'LL BE SURE TO CALL ON YOU DURING CLASS TODAY.
IN RETURN FOR YOUR LETTING ME STAY OVER.
WHAAAAT?!

HOW COME SHE ALWAYS CALLS ON ME?
FLOP
GOOD MORNING, HIDEKI! MORNING, CHI!
AND WHO IS THIS?

UH-
SHE-
THIS-
ER-
何と説明すれば
HOW DO I EXPLAIN?!
MY NAME IS TAKAKO SHIMIZU. I TEACH AT HIDEKI'S CRAM SCHOOL.
A TEACHER.
ぽん
THEN HIDEKI, YOU MUST HAVE GOTTEN A LOT OF **STUDYING** DONE LAST NIGHT.
UM-
THE-!
WHA-
BUT-
WE WERE DRINKING UNTIL DAWN!!
!?
ARE YOU GOING OUT TOO, CHI?
NO, SHE JUST WANTED TO WALK US OUT.
THAT'S SO SWEET.

HOW ARE YOU DOING FOR CLOTHES?
DOES CHI HAVE ENOUGH NOW?
CLAP
NOT QUITE.
I STILL HAVEN'T HAD A CHANCE TO GO SHOPPING FOR HER.
IF IT'S ALRIGHT WITH YOU, I COULD GIVE HER SOME MORE OUTFITS.
THAT'D BE **AWESOME!** THANK YOU SO MUCH!
COME ALONG, CHI. WE'LL FIND YOU **LOTS** OF NEW OUTFITS.
GO ON, CHI,
IT'S OKAY. MAKE SURE YOU DON'T BOTHER MS. HIBIYA.
UH HUH.

HAVE A GOOD DAY, HIDEKI.
IT WAS NICE MEETING YOU, MS. SHIMIZU.
HAVE A GOOD DAY!
GOODBYE!
YOUR LANDLADY'S PRETTY CUTE. YOU MUST FEEL LUCKY HAVING HER AROUND.
NOD
YEAH, MS. HIBIYA'S GREAT.
NOW, HIDEKI,
YOU DON'T WANT HER TO THINK WE'RE **GOING OUT**, DO YOU?
DON'T WORRY. IF SHE GETS THE WRONG IDEA, I'LL BE SURE TO DENY IT.
WHA- WHAT WRONG IDEA?

OF COURSE NOT, BUT SHOULDN'T **YOU** BE THE ONE WHO'S WORRIED?
YOU'RE **MARRIED**.
...YOU'RE RIGHT.
HEY, DIDN'T YOU HAVE SOMETHING YOU WANTED TO TALK TO ME ABOUT YESTERDAY?
HM?
TO BE HONEST, I WAS SO DRUNK LAST NIGHT I DON'T HAVE A CLUE WHAT IT WAS ABOUT.
BUT IF YOU CATCH ME WHEN I'M SOBER, I'D BE HAPPY TO TALK WITH YOU ABOUT WHATEVER.

OH, HIDEKI...
YOU REALLY ARE A GOOD GUY,
JUST LIKE THEY SAY.
EVEN IF YOU ARE A **VIRGIN.**
GRRRR!
DAMMIT!!
WHAT'S THAT GOT TO DO WITH ANYTHING!?

SEKI CRAM SCHOOL
SLUMP
PANT! PANT!
PHEW... MADE IT JUST IN TIME!
GOING TO SCHOOL WITH THE TEACHER HAS ITS PERKS... AT LEAST I CAN'T BE LATE.
YO!
SHIMBO.
ZZZZZZZZ
WHAT'S UP? YOU LOOK TIRED.
UHHH
I DIDN'T SLEEP A WINK.

WERE YOU STUDYING OR WHAT?
NAH, NOTHING LIKE THAT.
CLAK!
PLUM... WAKE UP, KIDDO.
...YES?
POKE POKE
YOU CAN GET OUT OF STANDBY MODE AND SHUT DOWN.
NIGHTY-NIGHT.
LET'S PLAY AGAIN LATER.
CURTSY
FLUTTER
FLOP!
WRIGGLE WRIGGLE

IS YOUR NOTEBOOK OKAY?
HER BATTERIES LOW OR SOMETHING?
SHE LOOKS WASTED.
UGH...
ZZZIP
POOR KID. PLUM WAS UP ALL NIGHT SEARCHING, TOO.
SEARCHING? FOR WHAT?
GOOD MORNING, CHILDREN!

I CAN'T BELIEVE SHE CAN STILL TEACH AFTER DRINKING SO MUCH...
I WISH I HAD THAT KIND OF TOLERANCE! EVEN BEFORE I PASSED OUT SHE HAD 12 BEERS AND 2 BOTTLES OF WINE.
WHAT'S SHIMBO LOOKING ALL PISSED ABOUT?

THIS IS MY ROOM. PLEASE COME IN.
THANK YOU FOR HAVING ME.
YOU'RE SO POLITE. DID HIDEKI TEACH YOU THAT?
UH HUH.
CLAK!
I'LL JUST BE A MOMENT.
CLICK

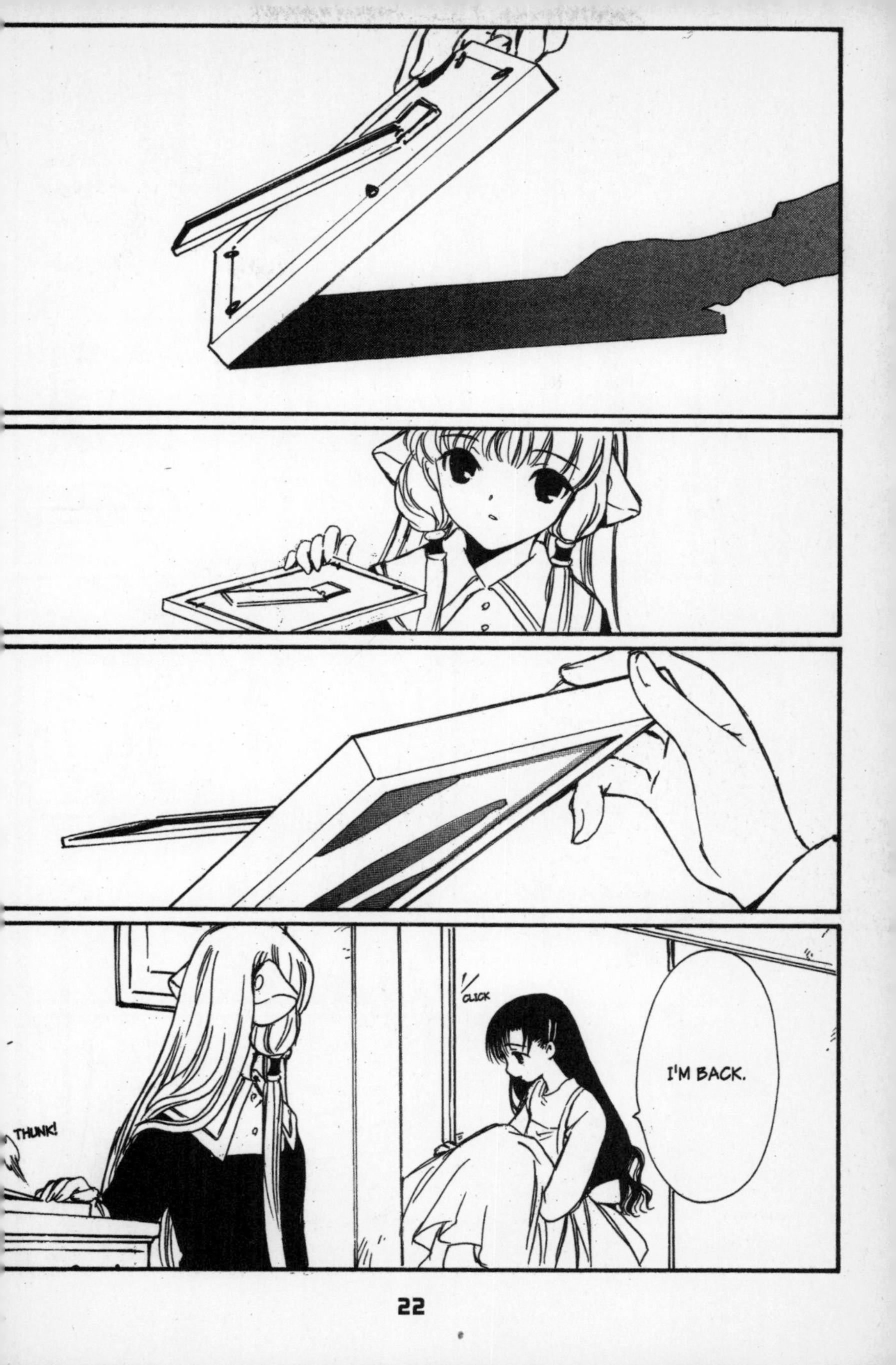

CLICK
I'M BACK.
THUNK!

WOULD YOU MIND TRYING THIS ON?
OKAY.
RUSTLE RUSTLE

HUG
I'M ALL CHANGED.
トン

WOW, THAT LOOKS GREAT ON YOU. A PERFECT FIT.
BUT OF COURSE IT WOULD BE.
THAT OUTFIT WAS MADE FOR YOU, AFTER ALL.
chapter.13 end

◀chapter.14▶

SEKI CRAM SCHOOL
関予備校
YAAAWWNN
AAHH...
IT'S FINALLY OVER. MAN, CLASS IS ROUGH WHEN YOU'VE GOT A HANGOVER.
WHAT'D YOU DO, STEAL A FEW DRINKS AFTER WORK? BOSS LET YOU HAVE A FEW ON THE HOUSE?
DUDE, YOU KNOW YOU CAN HOLD YOUR LIQUOR
NAH, IT WASN'T AT WORK, BUT I GUESS IT WAS STILL FREE BOOZE.
コキコキ
SHAKE SHAKE
ACTUALLY...
MS. SHIMIZU NEEDED A PLACE TO STAY LAST NIGHT SO SHE CRASHED AT MY PLACE AND GOT DRUNK.
WHISPER WHISPER
WHAAAAAT!
WAH!!
直撃!!
DIRECT HIT!

RING
DUDE, WATCH WHERE YOU'RE YELLING!
YOU DAMN NEAR GAVE ME A HEART ATTACK.
THMP THMP
TREMBLE
SHIMBO? WHAT ARE YOU SO PISSED ABOUT?
GRRR
SORRY.
I HAVE TO GO BACK TO THE SCHOOL.
TOK
TOK
HUH? WHY?
JUST GO ON WITHOUT ME!
DASH

...MS. SHIMIZU WAS LOOKING FOR SOME PLACE TO STAY LAST NIGHT...
...AND SHIMBO WAS UP ALL NIGHT LOOKING FOR SOME-THING...
HMM...
MAYBE WHAT SHIMBO WAS LOOKING FOR ...
...AND WHERE MS. SHIMIZU WAS GOING TO SPEND THE NIGHT ARE SOMEHOW...
CREEP

GUESS WHO!!
GRAB
GRURRRRGH!! YOU'RE-- CHOKING--ME!
I'M SORRY!!
FLOP
Y-YUMI?
SORRY ABOUT THAT. I MEANT TO COVER YOUR EYES.
IT'S NOT MY FAULT I'M SO SHORT I CAN ONLY REACH YOUR NECK!

PEEK
NO REALLY, ARE YOU OKAY? I'M SORRY.
むにっ
SMOOSH
WHOA! ARE THOSE HER BOOBS?
ER.... FORGET ABOUT BOOBS. JUST TELL HER YOU'RE FINE.
...Boobs!
STOP IT!
UNGH!
うっ
HIDEKI?
YES!
DON'T WORRY ABOUT TITS. YOU WERE JUST DOING YOUR BREASTS.
BEST... I MEAN BEST!!
AH!
URK!
にこっ
TEE HEE
DON'T WORRY ABOUT IT.
I GET THAT A LOT.

DUKLYON
HEY, HIDEKI.
HM?
YOU LIVE ALONE, DON'T YOU?
YEAH.
THAT'S WHY I ALWAYS BLURT OUT THE WRONG THING!
BUT YOU HAVE A **PERSOCOM** NOW, RIGHT?
YEAH.
THE ONE I FOUND.
SHAPED LIKE A GIRL?

IS SHE CUTE?
Y-YEAH.
OH YEAH!
SOMETIMES I WONDER ABOUT THAT...
HUH?
PERSOCOMS ARE ALL SO CUTE. ALL THE GUYS WHO GET ONE SEEM SO **ATTACHED** TO THEIRS.
I GUESS I'M A LITTLE **JEALOUS.**

YUMI...
HIDEKI, DO YOU THINK YOU'LL FEEL THAT WAY ABOUT **YOUR** PERSOCOM?
DO YOU THINK YOU'LL LIKE HER THE **BEST?**
THE BEST...
WHAT ARE YOU TALKING ABOUT?
I KNOW SHE'S CUTE AND ALL, BUT IT'S NOT LIKE SHE'S... SHE'S...
YES?

IT'S NOT LIKE SHE'S A REAL **PERSON**.
YOU REALLY FEEL THAT WAY?
YEAH, OF COURSE.
I'M SORRY! YOU MUST THINK I'M REALLY WEIRD.
THAT'S A RELIEF.
FOR A SECOND THERE, I THOUGHT SHE WAS GOING TO START CRYING.

CAN I HAVE A CHICKEN NUGGET?
I WONDER WHAT GOT HER SO WORKED UP.
SHE SAID SHE WAS JEALOUS THAT PERSOCOMS ARE SO CUTE...
AND THEN SHE SEEMED CONCERNED THAT I MIGHT HAVE FEELINGS FOR CHI...
AND SHE LOOKED SO RELIEVED WHEN I SAID NO.
COULD SHE... COULD SHE...
MIND IF I EAT SOME OF YOUR FRIES?
MAYBE, JUST MAYBE...?!
SLRP

YOU REALLY *HAVE* FORGOTTEN EVERYTHING.
WHAT DID CHI FORGET?
IT'S OKAY.
THAT'S WHAT HE WANTED.

YOU STILL HAVE YOUR DATA, DON'T YOU, CHI?
DATA?
YOU MEAN YOU DON'T HAVE IT?
HIDEKI SAID CHI HAS NO DATA.
SO IT'S BEEN LOST.
SLIP
HMM... PERHAPS IT'S FOR THE BEST. YOU MIGHT BE BETTER OFF IF THAT DATA IS NEVER INSTALLED.
CHI, DO YOU THINK YOU'LL FIND THE SOMEONE JUST FOR YOU?
CHI?

I HOPE YOU FIND HIM SOMEDAY.
SOMEONE WHO WILL LOVE **JUST YOU.**
THEN THE OTHER YOU WON'T BE NECESSARY ANYMORE.
◀chapter. 14▶ end

ちょびっツ
Chobits

chapter. 15

渡辺
パタン
CLAK
本須和
MOTOSUWA
SEE YOU TOMORROW.
TAKING OFF EARLY, EH, PART-TIMER?
LATER, MOTOSUWA.
YUMI! WHAT'S SHE DOING HERE?

HEY, YUMI. YOUR SHIFT'S OVER TOO?
YEAH.
I JUST WANTED TO THANK YOU FOR BUYING ME LUNCH TODAY. THAT WAS REALLY NICE.
OH...
IT WAS NOTHING. JUST FAST FOOD, Y'KNOW.
NO, REALLY. IT WAS GREAT!
SHAKE SHAKE
I MEAN...
...IT WAS GREAT BECAUSE IT WAS WITH **YOU.**

OH...
UM...
I WAS WONDERING...
ARE YOU DOING ANYTHING TOMORROW?
TOMORROW?
YOU DON'T HAVE SCHOOL, DO YOU?
WE COULD GO TO THE PARK, AND I'LL PACK US A NICE PICNIC LUNCH TO PAY YOU BACK FOR TODAY.
OH, YOU DON'T NEED TO WORRY ABOUT THAT.
HOW DID SHE KNOW THAT I DON'T HAVE SCHOOL?

IS SHE...
BADUM
IS SHE...
BADUM
GULP
I WAS RIGHT!
I'M SORRY. EVEN THOUGH YOU DON'T HAVE CLASS, I'M SURE YOU STILL HAVE TO STUDY. PLEASE FORGIVE ME. I DON'T KNOW WHAT I WAS THINKING--
ME STUDY?!
NO! NO! I'M NOT BUSY!!

REALLY?!
YUP. I'D LOVE TO JOIN YOU.
YAY!
HOP
IS 1:00 TOMORROW AT THE YAMATANI BOOKSTORE OKAY?
TOMORROW AT 1:00!
BYE!
OH! WHAT IF IT RAINS TOMORROW?

DON'T WORRY. IT'LL BE SUNNY! I JUST KNOW IT!
SEE YOU TOMORROW!!
SNEAK
YES!
I CAN'T BELIEVE IT!
YUMI ASKED ME
OUT ON A DATE!
NO FUCKING WAY!
DID SHE JUST..!?

I GUESS MY LUCK REALLY IS TURNING AROUND!
MY LANDLADY'S A FOX! MY TEACHER'S HOT! I'VE GOT A DATE WITH MY SEXY COWORKER!
WAHAHA!!
HMPH
MOTOSUWA?
I STILL DON'T BELIEVE IT.

AND I'VE GOT THE CUTEST PERSOCOM IN THE WORLD AND I DIDN'T HAVE TO PAY FOR HER!

LOOK AT THOSE TWO. REMINDS ME OF THIS GUY FROM WORK.

HE FELL HEAD OVER HEELS FOR HIS PERSOCOM AND NOW HE NEVER WANTS TO HANG OUT ANYMORE.

I KNOW SHE'S PRETTY, BUT NO MATTER WHAT SHE LOOKS LIKE, SHE'S STILL JUST A MACHINE.
HE SHOULD GET A LIFE, RIGHT?
CHI'S CUTE... MAYBE TOO CUTE.
BUT SHE'S STILL JUST AN ELECTRONIC APPLIANCE.
MACHINES AND PEOPLE ARE DIFFERENT.
AREN'T THEY?

CHI?
CHI!
WHAT THE HELL ARE YOU WEARING?!
WAAHH!
CHI'S CLOTHES ARE NO GOOD?
Y-YOUR PANTIES ARE SHOWING...
FLOP
THEY'RE ALMOST TOO GOOD!!
I'M SORRY, CHI. YOUR CLOTHES ARE FINE.
PAT

DID MS. HIBIYA GIVE THOSE TO YOU?
SHE HANDED THEM TO ME.
"MS. HIBIYA GAVE THEM TO ME"
IS FINE, CHI.
CHI?
HIDEKI SAID "GIVE" IS LIKE A GIFT FROM SOMEONE ELSE.
THAT'S RIGHT.
SO "MS. HIBIYA GAVE THEM TO ME" OR "I RECEIVED THEM FROM MS. HIBIYA" IS FINE.
BUT...
...SHE JUST HANDED THEM TO ME.
OH, YOU MEAN SHE "HANDED THEM OVER" TO YOU!
SHE GAVE YOU A LOT.
I BETTER THANK HER TOMORROW.

MUMBLE... BUT MS. HIBIYA CANNOT "GIVE" THIS DRESS. THIS WAS ALREADY CHI'S DRESS.
HIDEKI IS HAPPY?
IS IT THAT OBVIOUS?
I GUESS I'VE BEEN GLOWING EVERY SINCE I LEFT WORK.
FLOP
WHAT MAKES HIDEKI HAPPY?
CLATTER
I'M GOING OUT WITH SOMEONE FROM WORK TOMORROW.

SHE'S MAKING US A PICNIC LUNCH! OH, I WISH IT WOULD HURRY UP AND BE TOMORROW!
OH YEAH, I'VE GOT TO STUDY BEFORE WE GO OUT.
WHAT DO YOU CALL THAT?
I GUESS YOU WOULD CALL IT A **DATE**!
IS IT CALLED A DATE WHEN ANY TWO PEOPLE GO OUT TOGETHER?
NO! IT'S A DATE WHEN THE TWO PEOPLE... WHEN THEY HAVE **FEELINGS** FOR EACH OTHER.
FEELINGS?
IT MEANS TO LIKE EACH OTHER.

HI-
HIDEKI
LIKES THIS GIRL?
WELL, I DON'T KNOW HER ALL THAT WELL YET, BUT I THINK I LIKE HER.
SHE'S A GOOD KID!
AND SHE'S AN E-CUP!
HAVE TO FINISH THIS PAPER BEFORE TOMORROW!
chapter. 15 end

chapter.16

YUMI WAS RIGHT.. IT REALLY IS SUNNY.
SHE'S AMAZING.
I WONDER IF SHE HAD SOME PLACE IN MIND FOR US TO GO.
PROBABLY THE PARK OR SOMETHING SINCE SHE PACKED US LUNCH. ME AND YUMI, LAYING IN THE GRASS TOGETHER...
THIS IS GONNA BE GREAT!
Yamatani Bookstore
山谷書店
THIS IS THE PLACE.
10 TO 1:00! I'M JUST IN TIME.
I WOULDN'T WANT TO MAKE HER WAIT ON OUR FIRST DATE.
SEARCH
きょろきょろ
IT LOOKS LIKE SHE'S NOT HERE YET.

A City
With No People
someone just for me
OH...
THIS IS THE NEXT VOLUME OF THAT BOOK I BOUGHT FOR CHI, ISN'T IT?
FOR A PICTURE BOOK, IT SURE WAS HEAVY READING.
WERE PICTURE BOOKS THIS PHILOSOPHICAL WHEN I WAS A KID?

THERE'S NO ONE HERE EITHER.
JUST AS I FEARED...
A BEAUTIFUL DREAM...
...THAT NO ONE WANTS TO WAKE UP FROM.
THEY WILL GRANT YOUR DEEPEST WISHES.
EVERYONE IS INSIDE WITH *THEM.*
BEING WITH THEM IS LIKE LIVING A BEAUTIFUL DREAM.

THEY CAN DO THINGS THAT YOU CANNOT.
THEY WILL BE WHATEVER YOU WANT.
THEY WILL DO WHATEVER YOU ASK.
BUT...
THERE IS ONE THING...
...THEY CANNOT DO.
THEY CAN NEVER BECOME PEOPLE.
THEY MIGHT LOOK LIKE PEOPLE,
BUT THEY ARE ONLY SUBSTITUTES.
I KNOW THIS VERY WELL BECAUSE I AM ONE OF THEM.

TODAY I LOOK FOR SOMEONE JUST FOR ME.
SOMEONE WHO HAS LOVE FOR ME ALONE.
BUT...
SOMEONE WHO WILL LOVE ME EVEN IF I CAN'T FULFILL THEIR WISHES.
THERE IS ANOTHER ME.

THE OTHER ME ASKS...
DOES SUCH A PERSON EXIST?

I HOPE...
...SOMEONE WHO LOVES ME WITHOUT ASKING ANYTHING IN EXCHANGE.
I WANT...
...SOMEONE WHOSE LOVE FOR ME IS TRUE.
I NEED...
UNLESS THE SOMEONE LOVES ME FOR BEING ME...
...THEY'RE NOT SOMEONE JUST FOR ME.
IS THIS SO?
IT IS.
THIS SOMEONE EXISTS?
HE DOES.

...THEN WHERE?
IF SO...
MY SOMEONE IS NEARBY, I THINK. PERHAPS I ALREADY KNOW HIM.
BUT...
...WHAT IF THAT PERSON DOES NOT LOVE YOU BACK?

GUESS WHO!
SLAP
ぽん
GASP
HEY, YUMI. THANKS FOR NOT STRANGLING ME THIS TIME.
PHEW
YOU'RE EARLY.
I MEANT TO GET HERE FIRST
IT'S STILL 5 MINUTES TO 1:00.
A City With No People
YOU WERE READING A KIDS BOOK?
IS IT ANY GOOD?
YEAH. IT'S PRETTY WEIRD.
I'M NOT SURE IF IT'S GOOD OR WHAT.
YOU SURPRISE ME.
I NEVER WOULD HAVE GUESSED YOU LIKE PICTURE BOOKS.
IT'S NOT FOR ME...IT'S FOR CHI. SHE LIKES THE FIRST ONE.
CHI?

MY PERSOCOM BACK HOME.
SO YOUR YOU NAMED YOUR COMPUTER CHI?
YEAH.
SO! LET'S GET GOING!
GRAB
Y-YEAH!
YUMI GETS SAD WHENEVER WE TALK ABOUT PERSOCOMS.
I WONDER IF SHE HAD A BAD EXPERIENCE WITH THEM OR SOMETHING...

A City
People
FLIPE
A City With No People
PERK
vreen
CREAK
FLOAT

I CAN HEAR IT AGAIN.
SOMEONE IS CALLING ME.
WHO CAN IT BE?
chapter. 16 end

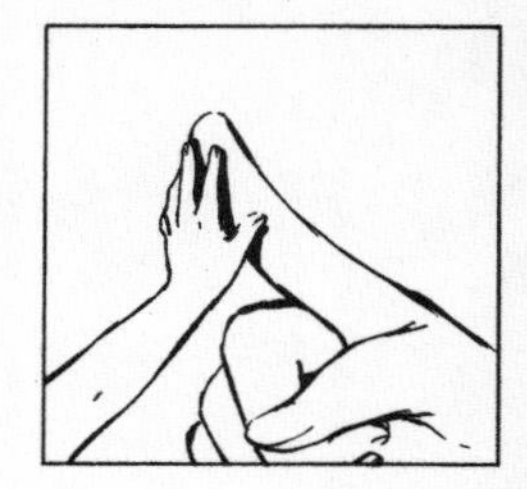

◀chapter.17▶

I NEVER EVEN KNEW THIS PLACE EXISTED.
CREAK
REALLY? I WAS WORRIED THAT GOING TO THE PARK WOULD BE TOO **ORDINARY**.
ARE YOU KIDDING? THIS IS GREAT!
I HAVEN'T BEEN BOATING IN YEARS.
I'M GLAD YOU LIKE IT!

I CAN'T BELIEVE IT! YUMI IS SOOO CUTE AND SHE'S GOING OUT WITH ME!
IT'S A BEAUTIFUL DAY...
WE'RE ALL ALONE...
CREAK
TODAY IS SHAPING UP TO BE...
YES!
...THE BEST DAY OF MY LIFE!
AH! HIDEKI, BEHIND YOU!
WHOOPS!

MINORU?!
WAVE
GOOD AFTERNOON.

WHAT ARE YOU DOING HERE?
IT'S THE WEEKEND.
I DO GET OUT, YOU KNOW.
BUT JUDGING BY YOUR FACE...
HUH
...I WOULD VENTURE THAT EXERCISE IS SOMETHING NEW TO YOU.

YOUR FRIEND... SHE'S A PERSON, ISN'T SHE?
HUH?
OF COURSE SHE IS! WHAT ELSE WOULD SHE BE?!
WITH THE NEW MODELS, IT'S HARD TO TELL WHO'S HUMAN THES DAYS.
I'M GLAD FOR YOU.
HUH?
CHI IS A LOVELY COMPANION.
I FIND IT ADMIRABLE THAT YOU HAVEN'T BECOME SO INVOLVED WITH YOUR PERSOCOM THAT YOU FORGET ABOUT PEOPLE.

YOU'RE THE LAST PERSON I'D EXPECT TO SAY THAT... BUT THANKS.
HEH HEH
YUMI WAS WORRIED ABOUT THAT TOO.
THAT I MIGHT PREFER MY PERSOCOM TO A REAL PERSON.
AND WHAT DID YOU TELL HER?
THAT COMPUTERS ARE DIFFERENT FROM PEOPLE.
THAT'S TRUE...
IT'S EASY TO FORGET.
THE MORE HUMAN OUR COMPUTERS BECOME...
...THE LESS WE FEEL THE NEED FOR TRUE HUMAN INTERACTION. BUT IT'S ALL A FACADE. OUR LOVE IS WASTED ON THEM.

THAT'S RIGHT.
WHEN I FIRST MET YOU...
...YOU WARNED ME NOT TO FALL IN LOVE WITH MY PERSOCOM.. THAT IT WOULD ONLY MAKE ME CRY..
WERE YOU--
...SPEAKING FROM EXPERIENCE? YES.
YOU FELL IN LOVE WITH YUZUKI, DIDN'T YOU?
WHAT MAKES YOU THINK THAT?
WELL,
THE WAY YOU LOOK AT HER, THE WAY YOU TALK TO HER...
IT'S DIFFERENT FROM HOW YOU TALK TO YOUR OTHER 'COMS.

I MEAN, UH--
I DIDN'T-- YOU DON'T HAVE TO ANSWER IF YOU DON'T WANT TO.
I'M BEING RUDE, AREN'T I?
WHAT'S SO SPECIAL ABOUT YUZUKI? YOU DON'T SEEM THE TYPE TO GO GAGA FOR A CUTE GIRL.
IS IT THAT OBVIOUS?
WELL... YEAH!
I...
AH...
UMMM...
HUH!?
?!
DO PEOPLE ALWAYS TELL YOU YOU'RE A GOOD GUY?
LET ME GUESS, MR. MOTOSUWA. EVERYONE TELLS YOU YOU'RE A NICE GUY, BUT AT THE END OF THE DAY, YOU'RE NEVER THE GUY WHO GOES HOME WITH THE GIRL.
STAB
DEAD ON
YOU DON'T HAVE TO RUB IT IN!!

I SUPPOSE I SHOULD TELL YOU...
TWO YEARS AGO MY SISTER DIED. SHE WAS THE ONLY FAMILY I HAD LEFT.
AND SO I BUILT YUZUKI.
SHE'S OUTWARDLY IDENTICAL TO MY SISTER, BUT THAT WASN'T ENOUGH.
I PROGRAMMED HER WITH ALL MY SISTER'S **MANNERISMS**, HER **LIKES** AND **DISLIKES**, ANYTHING I COULD REMEMBER.

IT WAS AN AMAZING SUCCESS.
IF YOU DIDN'T KNOW BETTER, YOU WOULD THINK YUZUKI WAS MY SISTER.
BUT BEHIND HER ACTIONS WAS NONE OF MY SISTER'S LOVE. TO YUZUKI, EVERYTHING IS JUST ONES AND ZEROES.
AS HER PROGRAMMER, I SHOULD UNDERSTAND THAT BETTER THAN ANYONE.
BUT WHEN SHE SMILES AT ME...
IT'S LIKE...
...MY SISTER NEVER LEFT.

SHE'S JUST A COMPUTER,
I KNOW.
THERE ARE TIMES WHEN I WISH I COULD FORGET THAT.
I HAVE FUN WITH YUZUKI,
BUT SOMETIMES I GET SAD AFTERWARDS. THE **MORE** FUN I HAVE, THE **SADDER** I GET.
THAT IS WHY I HAD TO WARN YOU.
I WOULDN'T WISH MY SORROWS ON ANYONE, MR. MOTOSUWA.
I APOLOGIZE IF I WAS MEDDLING.
I-I'M SORRY.
I DON'T KNOW WHAT TO SAY.
SCRATCH
S'OKAY. DON'T WORRY ABOUT IT.

PAT
YOU REALLY ARE A GOOD PERSON.
I HOPE THAT YOU LOSE YOUR VIRGINITY SOON.
HOW DO YOU KNOW ABOUT THAT?!!
DOH!
PAT PAT
WAS IT SHIMBO?! IT WAS SHIMBO, WASN'T IT! THAT FUCKER!
HE MENTIONED IT IN HIS LAST E-MAIL BLAST. I TAKE IT YOU WEREN'T ON THE CC LIST.
THEY LOOK LIKE THEY'RE HAVING FUN.
WHAT IS IT?
YOU'RE SO... BEAUTIFUL.

THANK YOU VERY MUCH.
...COMPUTERS ARE SO LUCKY.
THEY'RE PRETTY, INTELLIGENT, NICE...
HUMAN GIRLS JUST CAN'T COMPARE.
WHO IS CALLING?
IT IS ME.
WHO IS ME?

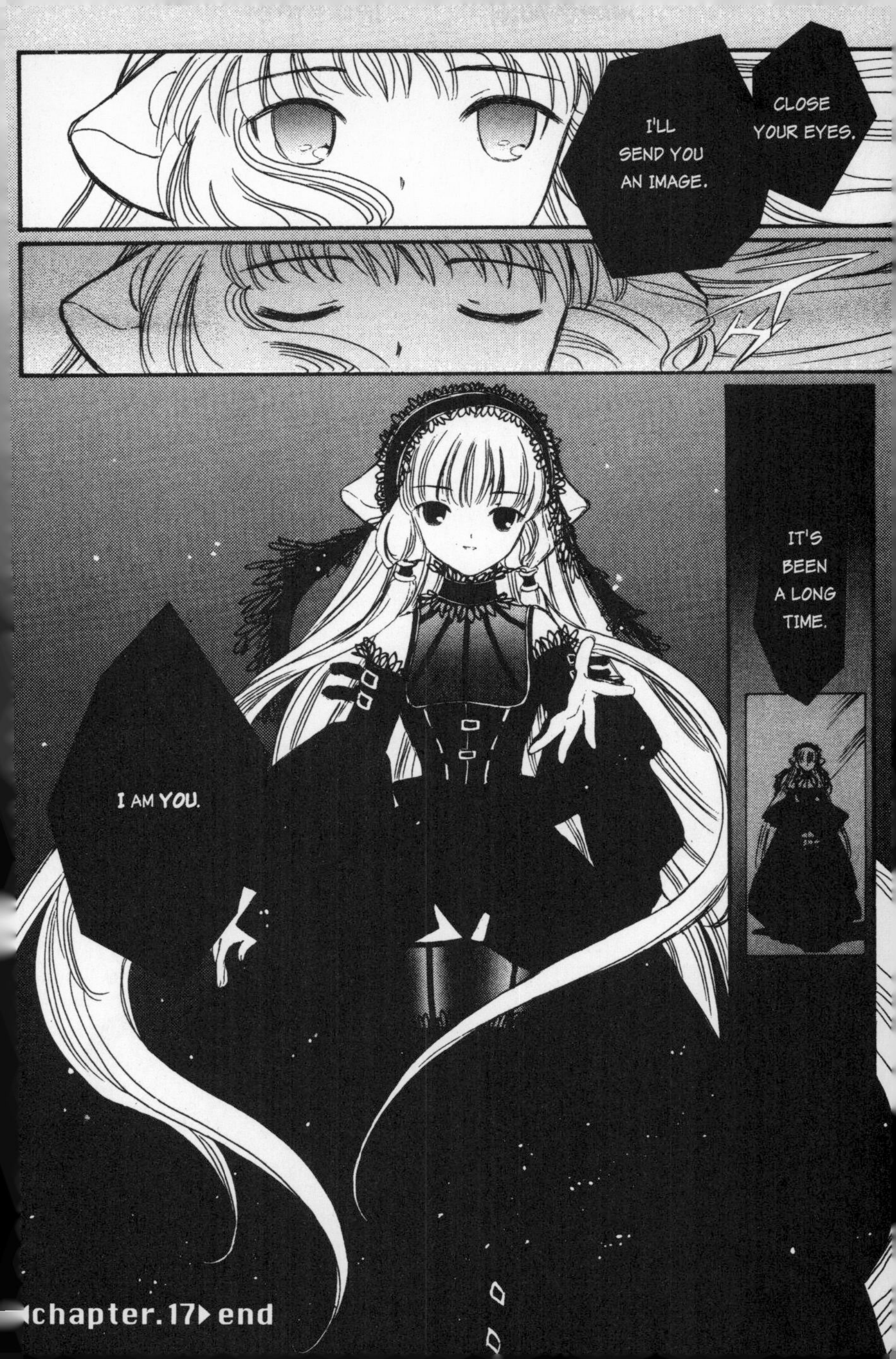
CLOSE YOUR EYES.
I'LL SEND YOU AN IMAGE.
IT'S BEEN A LONG TIME.
I AM YOU.
chapter.17 end

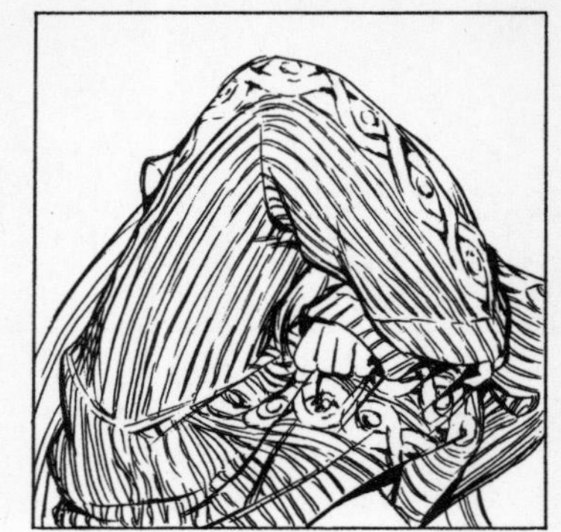

◂chapter.18▸

WERE YOU THE ONE CALLING ME?
WHY DO YOU HAVE THE SAME FACE AS ME?
I ALREADY TOLD YOU...
YES.
I WAS THE ONE CALLING YOU.
IT'S BECAUSE I'M YOU.

CHI DOESN'T UNDER-STAND.
SO, YOU'VE LOST ALL OF YOUR DATA.
THAT IS WHAT THE LANDLADY SAID.
THE LANDLADY?
CHITOSE HIBIYA.
SHE IS THE LANDLADY WHERE HIDEKI LIVES.
CHITOSE.
SO SHE'S CLOSE TO YOU

YOU KNOW THE LANDLADY?
I KNOW HER WELL.
NOW IT'S MY TURN TO ASK.
I KNOW **EVERYTHING**... EVEN THE THINGS YOU'VE FORGOTTEN.
WHO IS HIDEKI?
HIDEKI FOUND ME.
HE'S SOMEONE NEW.
SO, YOU GO BY CHI NOW?
CHI IS MY NAME.
HIDEKI NAMED ME.

IS THIS HIDEKI THE SOMEONE JUST FOR YOU?
SOMEONE JUST FOR ME...
SOMEONE WHO LOVES JUST YOU?
SOMEONE JUST FOR ME...
...I DON'T KNOW.
...I DON'T KNOW.
YOU REALLY HAVE FORGOTTEN EVERYTHING.

BUT I REMEMBER.
ABOUT US.
ABOUT WHAT WE HAVE TO DECIDE.
AND WHAT WE HAVE TO DO THEN.
IF **CHI** IS WHAT YOUR FRIEND CALLS YOU...
...I'LL CALL YOU **CHI**, AS WELL.
CHI.
WE'VE CONNECTED AGAIN.

FROM NOW ON...
EVERYTHING YOU DO, EVERYTHING YOU LEARN...
...WILL BE RELAYED TO ME.
YOU AND I ARE TOGETHER AGAIN.
TOGETHER FOREVER.
I'LL BE SEEING YOU,
CHI.

CHI!
WHAT ARE YOU DOING UP THERE?
I GOT WORRIED WHEN I CAME HOME AND YOU WEREN'T IN THE ROOM.
WELCOME HOME, HIDEKI.
THANKS. I'M GLAD YOU'RE OKAY.

RUSTLE
I BROUGHT YOU A PRESENT.
A BOOK.
A City With No People
SOMEONE JUST FOR ME - A CITY WITH NO PEOPLE
IT'S THE FOLLOW-UP TO THE OTHER BOOK I BOUGHT YOU. YOU SEEMED TO LIKE IT.
I'M SORRY! MAYBE I SHOULD HAVE BROUGHT YOU SOMETHING ELSE.
BUT YOU DON'T EAT SWEETS... I JUST DON'T KNOW WHAT TO GET FOR YOU.
WHAM
WHOA!

THUNK
THANK YOU,
HIDEKI.
SHWING!
I
-UH
YEAH-
I'M GLAD YOU LIKED IT.

THAT LOOK...
SHE WAS LIKE THAT AFTER I GAVE HER THE FIRST BOOK.
SHE LOOKS SO HAPPY.
LIKE SHE'S ABOUT TO CRY.
I KNOW SHE'S JUST A COMPUTER, BUT THOSE EMOTIONS ARE SO REAL.

ARE ALL PERSO-COMS LIKE THIS,
OR JUST CHI?
A City With No
BUT...
...WHAT IF THAT PERSON DOESN'T LOVE YOU BACK.
WHAT IF THAT PERSON LIKES SOMEONE...
...OTHER THAN YOU?

PEOPLE AREN'T EASY TO CHANGE.
PEOPLE AREN'T LIKE THEM.
YOU CAN'T ERASE THEIR FEELINGS.
I KNOW.

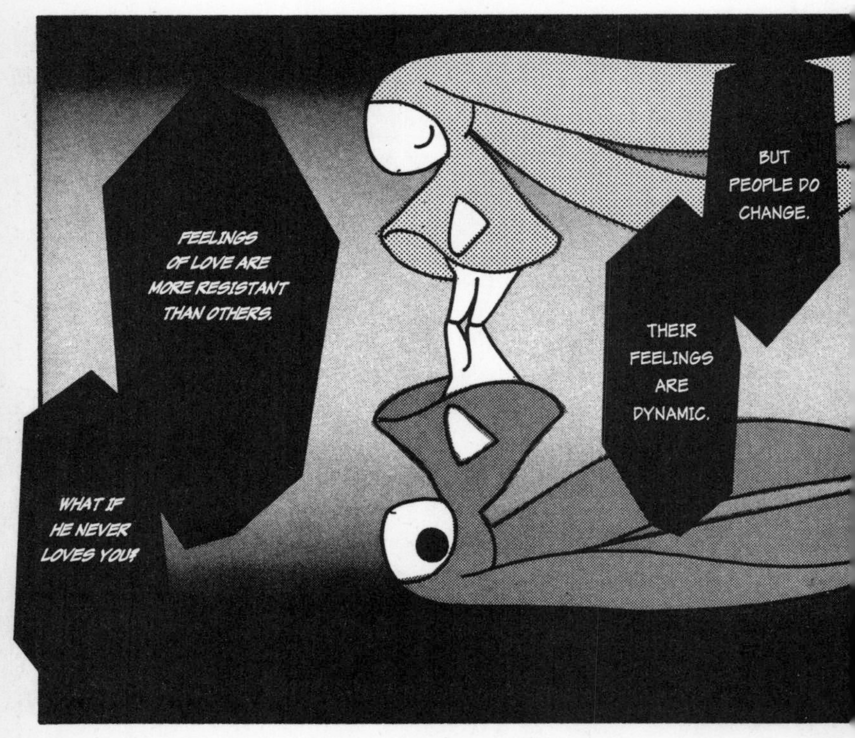
BUT PEOPLE DO CHANGE.
THEIR FEELINGS ARE DYNAMIC.
FEELINGS OF LOVE ARE MORE RESISTANT THAN OTHERS.
WHAT IF HE NEVER LOVES YOU?

THEN I'LL HAVE TO DECIDE.
A City
People
DECIDE....
...AND THEN DO WHAT MUST BE DONE.
ME AND THE OTHER ME.
hapter. 18 end
A City
People

◀chapter. 19▶

I DON'T GET IT!!
GRAARRH!!!
WHAT AM I GOING TO DO?!
I'VE BEEN STUDYING FOR TWO FUCKING YEARS!!
SLAM
HIDEKI!!
YUMI?

WHAT'S WRONG? YOU'RE STILL IN YOUR WORK CLOTHES.
たた
HUFF
居酒屋
よろこんぶ
GRAB
WHOA!
I'M SORRY TO BOTHER YOU WHILE YOU'RE STUDYING...
...BUT I REALLY WANTED TO SEE YOU.
D-DID SOMETHING HAPPEN AT WORK?
DID SOMEONE TRY TO TOUCH YOU?

SLIP
YOW!
SQEEZE
HOLD ME, HIDEKI...
BADUM BADUM
Y...
YUMI...

HIDEKI.
HUH?
WHAT THE?!
UNGH
I WANT YOU, HIDEKI.

M-
M-
M-
MS. SHIMIZU!
WHAT THE HELL IS GOING ON?!
...TAKE ME...

FOOM
FAINT
ARE YOU THE SOMEONE JUST FOR ME?
OR IS THERE SOMEONE ELSE YOU LIKE?
WHICH IS IT?
TELL ME, HIDEKI.
HIDEKI...

HIDEKI...
HIDEKI...
HUH?
AH...
ぱち
SNAP
HIDEKI KEPT MOVING AND MAKING NOISES IN HIS SLEEP.
IS HIDEKI OKAY?
I WAS HAVING A NIGHT-MARE.
A NIGHT-MARE?

HMMMM... HOW DO I EXP-LAIN?
A NIGHTMARE IS LIKE A SCARY DREAM.
HIDEKI HAD A SCARY DREAM?
ACTUALLY...
IT WAS PRETTY GOOD UNTIL ABOUT HALFWAY THOUGHT...
IT WAS A LITTLE SCARY.
BUT I'M OKAY! IT WAS JUST A DREAM!

CHI DOESN'T HAVE DREAMS.
CHI DOESN'T UNDERSTAND.
OH...
SHE'S A COMPUTER. OF COURSE SHE WOULDN'T UNDERSTAND WHAT A DREAM IS.
DREAMS AREN'T REAL. THEY CAN'T HURT YOU.
SEE, I'M FINE!
IS HIDEKI OKAY DOWN THERE TOO?
WHAAAAAA!!

KEEP IT QUIET...
CHI?

PHEW!
WHAT AN EXCITING MORNING!
I COULDN'T HELP IT AFTER A DREAM LIKE THAT.
EMPTY
SIGH

EMPTY
WHAT ARE YOU DOING, HIDEKI?
SIGH...
NO MATTER HOW MANY TIMES I CHECK, THERE'S NO MONEY!
MONEY?
YEAH. IT'S WHAT YOU USE TO BUY THINGS. EVEN IF YOU BUY STUFF ONLINE, YOU STILL HAVE TO HAVE MONEY. IT'S JUST DIGITAL... OR SOMETHING.
SHIMBO SAID SOMETHING ABOUT THAT.
I DON'T KNOW WHAT TO DO. IT'S NOT LIKE I CAN PUT IN MORE HOURS AT MY JOB.
JOB?

YOU KNOW, WORK.
WHY DOES HIDEKI HAVE TO WORK?
YOU WORK TO GET MONEY. YOU NEED MONEY TO LIVE. THAT'S THE GAME.
CLINCH
I DON'T KNOW HOW I'M GONNA AFFORD THOSE TEXTBOOKS.
AT LEAST I CAN BORROW PORNO DVDS FROM MY BOSS.
SCORE
CHI WILL GET A JOB.
EH?

CAN CHI DO THIS JOB?
LADIES!
Become the girl of men's DREAMS and earn big MONEY!
NOW HIRING NEW MODELS!
Call Now! It's fast and easy. No Experience Necessary
SURGE
CHI?
WAAAA
HERE WE GO AGAIN!

◂chapter. 19▸ end

◀chapter.20▶

CLUB PLEASURE
WHERE AM I GONNA FIND THE RIGHT KIND OF JOB?
CLUNK
HIDEKI!
OH, HEY, YUMI.
YOU DONE ALREADY?
YES!!

I CAN'T LOOK HER IN THE FACE.
BLUSH
NOT AFTER THAT DREAM I HAD THIS MORNING.
ARE YOU HAVING PROBLEMS AT WORK?
HUH?!
WHY DO YOU ASK?!
I JUST OVERHEARD YOU TALKING WHEN I CAME IN.
SOMETHING ABOUT FINDING A JOB.
AAAAARRHH!
I WAS TALKING TO MYSELF AGAIN!!
SO EMBARRASSING! I'VE GOT TO STOP DOING THAT!

UM...
YOU AREN'T THINKING OF QUITTING THIS JOB...
ARE YOU?
FLAP FLAP
NO, OF COURSE NOT! IF I QUIT MY JOB, HOW COULD I AFFORD TO BUY STUFF?!
I'M GLAD.
OH!
YUMI HAS SUCH A GREAT SMILE.

WAIT A MINUTE... WHY'S SHE SO WORRIED ABOUT ME LEAVING?
COULD SHE BE...
ちら
SHE'S WORRIED ABOUT ME!!
HOOYA!
THEN WHAT JOB WERE YOU TALKING ABOUT?
IT'S FOR CHI.
CHI'S YOUR PERSOCOM, RIGHT?

SHE SAID SHE WANTS TO GET A JOB.
SHE'S SMART AND ALL, BUT I MEAN, IT'S NOT LIKE SHE HAS ANY REAL WORLD EXPERIENCE.
I DON'T KNOW WHAT SHE WOULD DO.
YUMI?
PERSOCOMS CAN DO ANYTHING YOU PROGRAM THEM TO.
I'M SURE SHE CAN GET ANY JOB SHE WANTS.
YEAH, I GUESS YOU'RE RIGHT.
IT DEFINITELY BOTHERS HER WHEN WE TALK ABOUT PERSOCOMS.

WHAT COULD HAVE HAPPENED TO HER?
IN ANY CASE, I SHOULD BE MORE CAREFUL.
I'M SO CLUELESS.
RUSTLE
OH, I ALMOST FORGOT! I BAKED COOKIES.
HERE!
TADA
F-FOR ME?!
SHE BAKED COOKIES FOR ME?
I TRIED THEM OUT, AND I THINK THEY'RE OKAY. I HOPE YOU LIKE THEM.

OH!
MAYBE YOU DON'T LIKE THIS KIND. IF YOU DON'T LIKE THEM, I COULD--
LIKE THEM? ARE YOU KIDDING, I *LOVE* THEM!
THANKS
THE LUNCH YOU MADE WAS GOOD TOO. I'M SURE THESE WILL BE GREAT!
SEE YOU!
TAKE CARE!
PATTER

THIS IS IT! THIS IS FOR REAL.
A GIRL DOESN'T GO AND BAKE YOU COOKIES IF SHE DOESN'T LIKE YOU, RIGHT?
にこっ
BEAM
祐巳ちゃんのクッキー♪
HOMEMADE COOKIES, OH YEAH!
手作りクッキー♪
COOKIES FROM YUMI!

SWEEP
HELLO, CHI.
HELLO.
FLOAT

ARE YOU GOING OUT TODAY?
CHI IS GOING TO FIND A JOB.
YOU ARE? WHY WOULD YOU DO A THING LIKE THAT?
CHI KNOWS JOBS ARE FOR MAKING MONEY. HIDEKI NEEDS MORE MONEY.
SO YOU'RE DOING IT FOR HIDEKI?
FOR HIDEKI?
CHI CAN'T GO TO WORK FOR HIDEKI.
NO, I MEAN YOU'RE DOING IT FOR HIDEKI'S BENEFIT. TO HELP HIM?
CHI?

TO MAKE HIM HAPPY.
WHEN HIDEKI'S HAPPY, CHI FEELS HAPPY TOO.
PAT
I WONDER IF HIDEKI IS THE ONE WHO WILL LOVE YOU.
I DON'T KNOW.

WOULD IT MAKE YOU HAPPY IF HE DID?
CHI... CHI DOESN'T KNOW.
YOU'LL KNOW. IF HE'S THE ONE, YOU'LL KNOW.
GOOD LUCK, CHI. AND BE CAREFUL!
THANK YOU! I WILL.
I HOPE YOU FIND THE SOMEONE JUST FOR YOU, CHI.
I REALLY DO.
JUST LIKE HE WISHED.

TAP
EXCUSE ME, MISS!
YOU'RE A PERSOCOM.
WHAT'S A GREAT-LOOKING MODEL LIKE YOU DOING OUT ALONE? WHERE'S YOUR OWNER?
CHI IS LOOKING FOR A JOB.
A JOB, EH?
TODAY'S YOUR LUCKY DAY! I'VE GOT JUST THE JOB FOR YOU...
chapter.20 end

◀chapter.21▶

ぽつん
ALONE
CLACK
ARE YOU FINISHED CHANGING, CHI?
WOW, YOU'RE A KNOCKOUT!
I DID A LITTLE LOOKING AROUND, BUT I COULDN'T FIND ANYONE WHO MAKES YOUR MODEL.
ARE YOU A CUSTOM JOB?
WHO MAKES YOU?
CHI?

HEY, HEY! DO YOU THINK THE GUY WHO BUILT YOU COULD MAKE ME ANOTHER ONE OF YOU?
THERE IS...
...ONE OTHER WHO LOOKS LIKE CHI.
REALLY?! IS SHE FOR SALE? YOU'VE GOTTA INTRODUCE ME TO THE GUY WHO MADE YOU!
CHI DOESN'T KNOW WHO MADE HER.
YOUR OWNER MADE YOU, RIGHT?
SHAKE
NO.
HIDEKI'S MY OWNER.
HE **FOUND** ME.
HE DIDN'T **MAKE** ME.

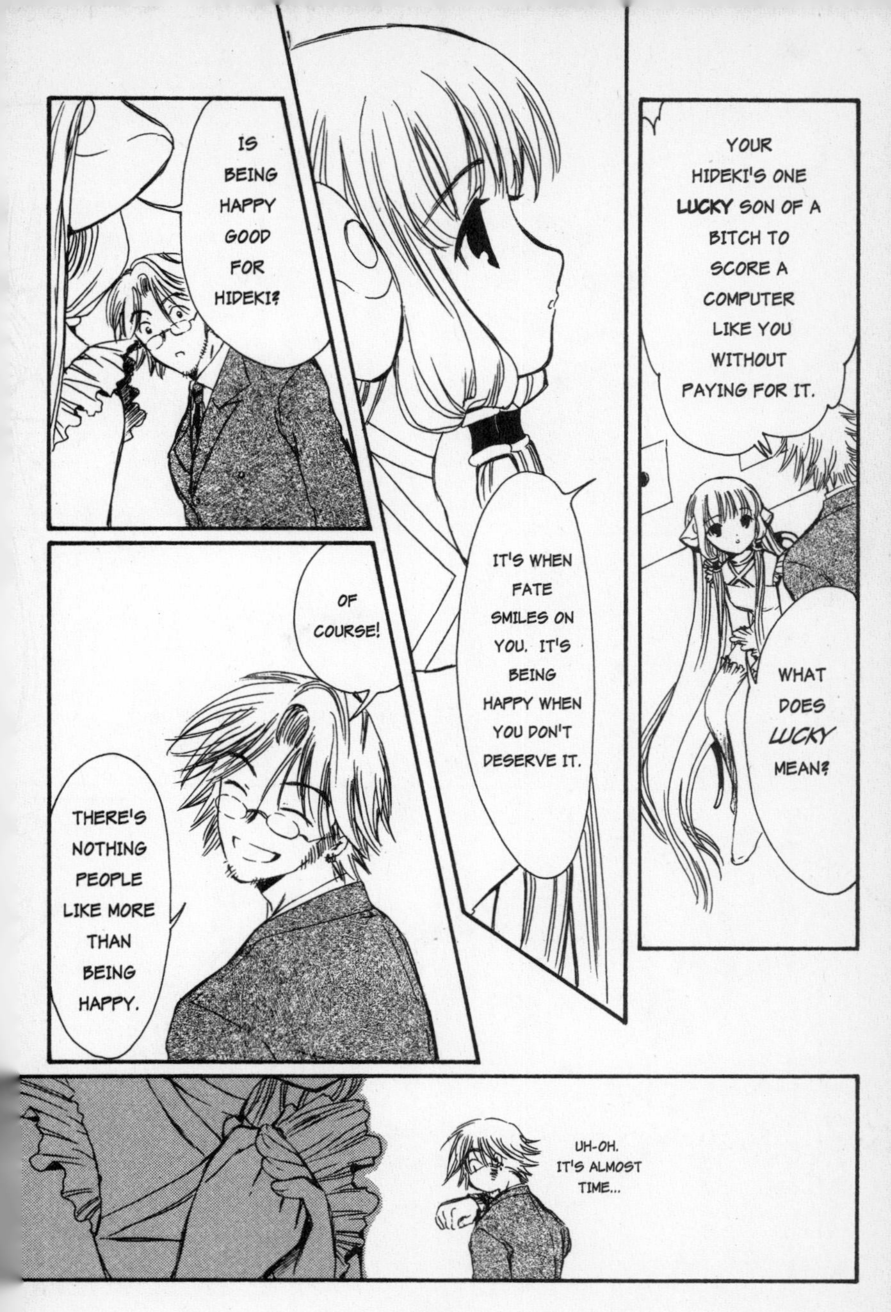
YOUR HIDEKI'S ONE LUCKY SON OF A BITCH TO SCORE A COMPUTER LIKE YOU WITHOUT PAYING FOR IT.
WHAT DOES LUCKY MEAN?
IT'S WHEN FATE SMILES ON YOU. IT'S BEING HAPPY WHEN YOU DON'T DESERVE IT.
IS BEING HAPPY GOOD FOR HIDEKI?
OF COURSE!
THERE'S NOTHING PEOPLE LIKE MORE THAN BEING HAPPY.
UH-OH. IT'S ALMOST TIME...

FINDING CHI...
...MADE HIDEKI...
...HAPPY.

OK, BABY, LET'S ROLL!
WHAT SHOULD CHI DO?
SLIP
JUST SIT THERE AND TAKE YOUR CLOTHES OFF.
JUST TAKE THEM OFF?
YEAH, AND EVERY ONCE IN A WHILE...
LIKE THIS!
...STRIKE A SEXY POSE FOR THE CUSTOMERS. YOU'RE A STAR, BABY. MAKE IT LOOK GOOD.
CUSTOMERS?
YUP!

YOU DIDN'T THINK I'D PAY FOR YOU TO STRIP IN PRIVATE, DID YOU?
RIGHT ON THE OTHER SIDE OF THOSE HOLES, YOUR FANS ARE WAITING!
SEE YA LATER!
SLAM
ぱたん
とこ とこ とこ とこ とこ
PIT PAT
PIT PAT
SHWUMP
CHI?
SWIRL
ぐりぐり

I WAS ON COOKING DUTY TODAY, SO MY BOSS GAVE ME FOOD TO TAKE HOME!
I MADE YAKITORI AND MEATBALLS.
NOT BAD, IF I DO SO SAY MYSELF.
CLIK
I'M HOME!
MAYBE SHE'S UP ON THE LAMP AGAIN?
NOPE NOT THERE...

CHIII!
WHOOSH
WHERE COULD SHE HAVE GONE?
KNOCK KNOCK
UH... COME IN!

HELLO, HIDEKI. I WAS JUST MAKING DINNER AND I HAD EXTRA.
WOULD YOU LIKE SOME?
SURE THING. THANK YOU VERY MUCH.
UH, MS. HIBIYA,
I DON'T SUPPOSE YOU KNOW WHERE CHI IS?
SHE'S NOT IN MY ROOM.
SHE WENT OUT ABOUT AN HOUR AGO.
SHE SAID SHE WAS LOOKING FOR A JOB.
WHHHAAAA?!
SHE WAS SERIOUS?!

ARE YOU GOING OUT TOO?
I'VE GOTTA GO FIND HER!
STOMP
STOMP
DASH
HAVE FUN, HIDEKI.
OH, CHI... WOULDN'T IT BE NICE IF HIDEKI WAS THE SPECIAL PERSON JUST FOR YOU?

WHAT WERE YOU THINKING, CHI?!
SEARCH
きょろきょろ
SHE DOESN'T KNOW ANY-THING ABOUT THE WORKING WORLD. HOW DOES SHE EXPECT TO FIND A JOB?
REPLAY
CAN CHI DO THIS JOB?
LADIES!
Become the girl of men's DREAMS and earn big MONEY!
Now Hiring New Models!
YOU PROBABLY COULD. I'M SURE GUYS WOULD PAY TO SEE YOU--
しずかに しずかに
SCHUCKA SCHUCKA
WHAT AM I TALKING ABOUT, NO!!
CHI?
DON'T TELL ME SHE REALLY WENT FOR A JOB LIKE THAT!
DASH

HUH?
IT'S SHIMBO.
HEY, SHI--
WAIT!
I'LL MAKE HIM HELP ME FIND CHI.
MAYBE LAPTOP CAN HELP LOCATE HER.
ZOOM
WHO'S HE TALKING TO?

◀chapter.21▶ end

chapter.22

TRY TALKING.
MI-NO-RU.
SPEECH ABILITY CHECK COMPLETE.
THE ONLY THING WE HAVE LEFT IS YOUR CPU CHECK.

DON'T YOU NEED TO BACK UP MY **MEMORY FILES?**
AND WE HAVEN'T INPUT THE NEW **BEHAVIOR PATTERNS** FOR YOUR SISTER...
WELL... UH...
YUZUKI.
ABOUT THAT...
YES?
FROM NOW ON--

PING
WHAT'S THIS?
WHAT IS IT MINORU?
IT'S CHI. I LEFT THE SEARCH PROGRAM RUNNING. IT MUST HAVE FOUND SOMETHING ON HER.
M
YUZUKI, CAN YOU SWITCH TO VISUAL?
YES.
FLASH

OH, DEAR...
THAT'S CHI?
BLIP
BLIP
BUT THAT IS MOST DEFINITELY **NOT** MR. MOTOSUWA'S ROOM.
BLIP
HER OUTWARD APPEARANCE MATCHES...
BLIP
CAN YOU TRACE THE SIGNAL? SEE WHERE IT'S AIRING FROM?
JUST A MOMENT.
FOOSH

IT'S COMING FROM AN ENTERTAINMENT ESTABLISHMENT CALLED *LIVE PEEP*.

COME SEE THE LATEST GIRLFRIEND, CUTE KITTY NYAN NYAN. I BROUGHT THIS STRAY IN OFF THE STREETS AND NOW SHE'S PUTTING ON A SENSUAL PURR-FORMANCE FOR YOU. WATCH HER DRESS-UP ANTICS AND GIVE MISS KITTY SOME MILK.

HMM

MILK

DRESS-UP

ANTICS

CUTE KITTY NYAN NYAN

PURR-FORMANCE

DOES HIDEKI KNOW ABOUT THIS?

I CAN'T IMAGINE THAT HIDEKI WOULD PUT HIS PERSOCOM UP FOR SOMETHING LIKE THIS.

YEAH, BABY, THAT'S IT!

KEEP TAKING IT OFF.

OKAY

NO, NO! DON'T LOOK AROUND. LOOK SEXY! THE CUSTOMERS CAN'T HEAR ME.

CUMMON, BABY, LET'S SEE SOME MORE ACTION. YOU'RE ON A LIVE WEBCAST. SHOW THE VIEWERS WHAT THEY WANNA SEE.

YEAH, YEAH. REAL NICE. YOU SHOW 'EM YOUR LEGS, NOW SHOW 'EM A LITTLE TOPSIDE.

SLIP

THAT'S RIGHT. TEASE THEM A BIT, THEN LOSE THE BRA.

HEY, HEY...
CHI?
TUG
STRETCH
WHAT'S THE MATTER? YOU DON'T KNOW HOW TO TAKE OFF A BRA?
CHI NEVER WORE ONE OF THESE BEFORE.
YOUR OWNER DIDN'T HAVE YOU WEAR ONE?
KINKY
ALRIGHT, ALRIGHT, WE'LL SAVE THAT FOR LATER. GO FOR THE PANTIES NOW.
PANTIES, PANTIES.
SLIP
THAT'S WHAT I'M TALKING ABOUT.

WE DON'T WEAR PANTIES ON OUR HEADS. HIDEKI TOLD ME, SO I KNOW.
STRETCH
YEAH, BABY, THAT'S FASCINATING. NOW, USE YOUR **FINGER** TO UP THE EXCITEMENT.
FINGER?
YEAH. START PLAYING WITH YOUR-SELF.
WHERE?
BETWEEN YOUR LEGS, BABY. DO I HAVE TO SPELL IT OUT?
STOP
IF THIS WASN'T JUST A STRIP SHOW, I'D TOUCH YOU MYSELF.
NO.
HUH?
WHY NOT?

NO.
CHI CAN'T TOUCH THERE.
WHAT'S THAT? I CAN'T FUCKING HEAR YOU.
NO!
CHI'S SPOT...
...CAN'T BE TOUCHED.

THAT'S RIGHT, CHI.
YOU WERE RESTARTED BY THAT SWITCH.
THAT'S WHY...

...UNTIL YOU FIND THE SOMEONE WHO LOVES YOU...

...NO ONE CAN TOUCH YOU THERE.

AND, CHI...

THE NEXT TIME YOU GET TOUCHED THERE...
...IT'S FOR US TO DECIDE.

SOME-THING'S NOT RIGHT, MINORU...
ZOOM IN ON HER FACE.
OKAY.
chapter.22 end

◂chapter.23▸

CLACK
CLACK
WHAT THE HELL ARE YOU DOING? WE'RE LOSING THE FUCKING CUSTOMERS.
HERE, I'LL **SHOW** YOU.

JUST STICK YOUR FINGER RIGHT HERE,
AND--
RRK
PSHING!

WHAT'S SHIMBO DOING WITH MS. SHIMIZU?
NO, THAT'S NOT IT.
THERE'S DEFINITELY A CRAZY, SERIOUS VIBE HERE.
SHUFFLE
すすすす
LOOK, HE'S HIDING!
DOES HE HAVE A QUESTION ABOUT CLASS? OR MAYBE THEY JUST WENT OUT FOR A DRINK?

SHE'S CRYING!
SHE...
BRUSH
...DON'T CRY.

I'M NOT CRYING.
THEN WHY ARE MY CLOTHES GETTING WET?
TUG
IT MUST BE RAINING.
DAMMIT. CAN'T YOU BE HONEST WITH YOURSELF?
I'M NOT HONEST, I'M NOT CUTE. I'M NO ONE.
SIGH

YOU *ARE SO* CUTE.
YOU'RE *AMAZINGLY* CUTE.
I CAN'T BELIEVE HOW CUTE YOU ARE!
...OH, LOOK.
I RUBBED MY MAKEUP ALL OVER YOU. I'M SORRY.
YOU CAN RUB ALL YOU WANT, BUT WILL YOU JUST *SHUT UP* FOR A MINUTE?
YES?

I'M SUCH A SUCKER FOR A WOMAN IN DISTRESS.
ANY WOMAN?
GRAB
YOU'RE THE BEST, BABY.
WAIT... SOMEONE MIGHT SEE US.
←まさに見ている
TOTALLY SEEING THEM.
April
WE NEED TO TALK. AS SOON AS I BROUGHT IT UP, YOU RAN AWAY.
I KNEW WHAT YOU WERE GOING TO SAY. I JUST COULDN'T STAND TO HEAR YOU SAY IT.

SHOULD I BE WATCHING THIS?
YOU DON'T KNOW EVERY-THING.
YES... I DO...
I KNOW I SHOULDN'T.
I KNOW--
I KNOW, BUT...!!
I JUST CAN'T PULL MY EYES AWAY!!!

SHAKE SHAKE
YOU'VE GOT MAIL!
SLUMP
CRASH
I FORGOT TO TURN HER OFF.
I WAS USING HER TO FIND YOU.
YOU'VE GOT MAIL! IT'S FROM MINORU KOKUBUNJI!
SHALL I READ IT TO YOU?
NOT **NOW**, PLUM!
BUT WHAT IF IT'S AN EMERGENCY? YOU SHOULD LISTEN TO IT.

GO AHEAD AND READ IT, PLUM.
OKEY DOKEY.
HELLO, SHIMBO. IT'S KOKU-BUNJI.
VREEEN
SHE'S READING IN KOKU-BUNJI'S VOICE!!
I'M SORRY TO BOTHER YOU LIKE THIS,
BUT DO YOU KNOW WHERE HIDEKI IS?
IT'S ABOUT CHI...
LAPTOPS CAN DO THAT? IT'S SO CREEPY!
POOWSH
WHAT ABOUT CHI?!

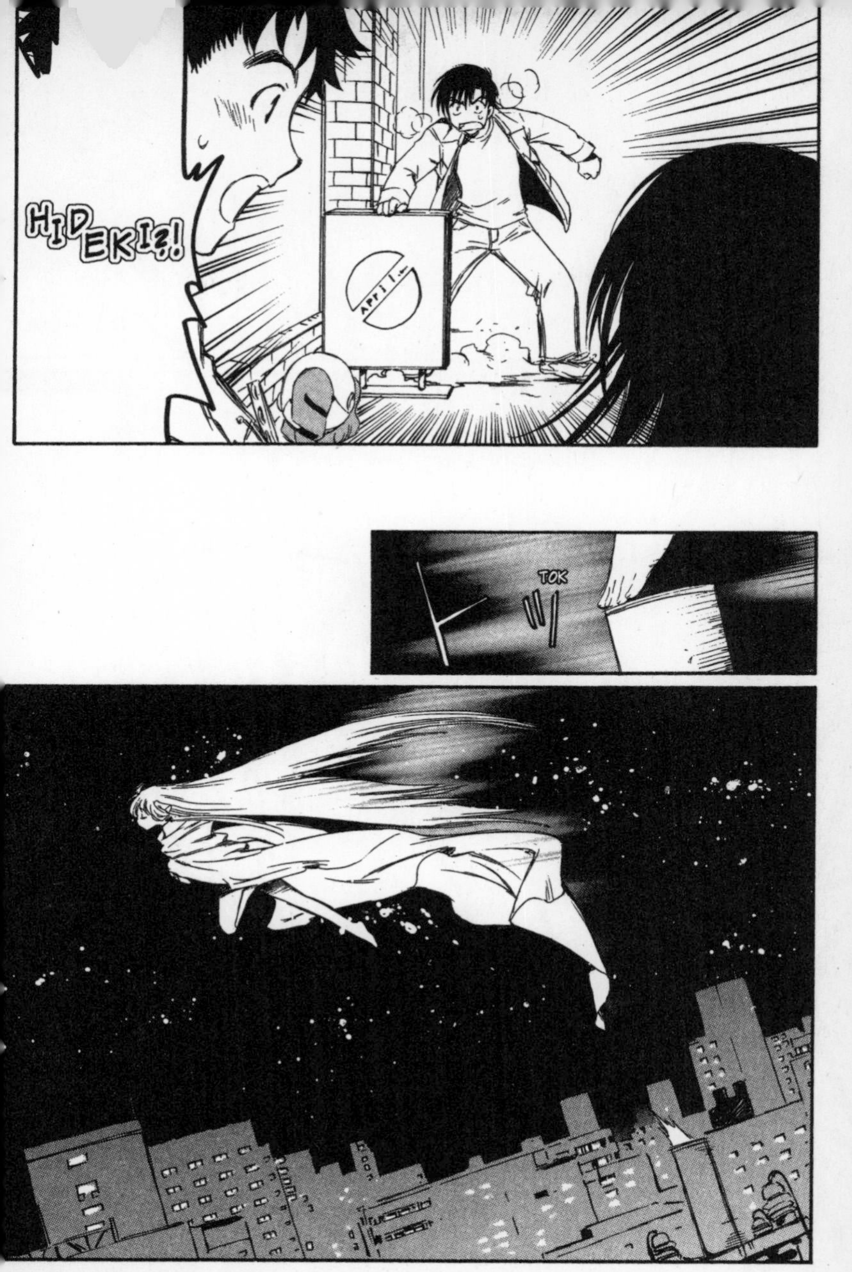

◀chapter.23▶ end

◀chapter.24▶

HUH?
WHAT THE?
FLOAT
VREEEN

HEY, WHAT'S GOING ON?!
WHY DID YOU STOP?
WHAT'S WRONG?

WA-WA-
WHAT ARE
YOU DOING
HERE?!
SNATCH
ASK ME
LATER!
WHAT
ABOUT CHI?
TELL ME!
ROOOAR
SHE'S PERFORMING
IN A RATHER SHADY
PEEP SHOW,
AND I WAS
WONDERING IF HIDEKI
WAS AWARE.
A
PEEP
SHOW!?!
ROAR!
YOU'RE
MAKING
CHI DO
THAT?
THAT'S
LOW,
DUDE.
ARGH!!
SHAKE
I'M
NOT!

END OF MESSAGE!
WHERE IS THE PEEP SHOW?!
MASTER, HE'S SCARING ME.
DON'T KILL THE MESSENGER, DUDE. SHE'S ONLY READING THE E-MAIL. IT'S NOT LIKE SHE KNOWS.
AH!
AH!
AH!
WHAT AM I SUPPOSED TO DO!
I WON'T LET THE SCARY MAN HURT YOU.
'KAY
WHY DON'T YOU TRY CALLING?
GASP
OF COURSE!!

I NEED A PHONE! WHAT'S MINORU'S NUMBER?!
PANIC
あたふた
WHERE'S THE PAY PHONE?!
PANIC
あたふた
PAY PHONE? GET WITH THE FUCKING CENTURY, DUDE!
HE DOESN'T EVEN HAVE A CELL PHONE?
CAN PLUM MAKE PHONE CALLS?
OF COURSE. WIRELESS MODEM.
SCARY!
こわーい
GRIP
LET ME BORROW HER!

THMP THMP THMP
RING RING! RING RING!
MINORU! ANSWER THE PHONE, DAMMIT!
DASH
DASH DASH
I'VE GOT A BAD FEELING ABOUT THIS. MAYBE I SHOULDN'T HAVE LENT HIM PLUM.
HE BETTER NOT DROP HER, RUSHING AROUND LIKE THAT.
I THINK IT'S ROMANTIC.

HUH?
IF I WAS IN TROUBLE, I'D LOVE TO HAVE THE GUY I LIKE SEARCH FOR ME WITH THAT KIND OF PASSION.

DASH
CLICK
HELLO, KOKUBUNJI HERE.
THAT VOICE! MINORU!
WHERE'S CHI?! IS SHE STILL AT THAT PEEP SHOW?!

NO.
SHE'S MOVED.
H
WHERE TO?!
I DON'T KNOW, BUT YOU'D BETTER FIND HER QUICKLY. SHE'S ACTING STRANGE.
WHAT DO YOU MEAN, STRANGE!?
RIGHT AFTER THE MAN AT THE PEEP SHOW TRIED TO TOUCH HER--
CLICK
VROOON

GASP
YUZUKI?!
VREEEN

MINORU?! MINORU!?!
SHE'S DISCONNECTED!?
どうなってんだー
おいーっ!!
vreeen
DEAR, WHAT'S WRONG?
C'MON, CAN'T YOU MOVE, PLEASE?!
buzz buzz
SOME-ONE HELP!
MY PERS-OCOM...!
DID SOMETHING HAPPEN?
GASP

CHI?!

CHI!
CHI!
CAN YOU HEAR ME?!
SHOVE
CHI!!
HI-
-DE
-KI

VREEEN
FLOAT
WHAT IS THE MATTER, SIR?
WHAT DO YOU MEAN, *WHAT'S THE MATTER?!* YOU SCARED ME HALF TO DEATH, SHUTTING OFF LIKE THAT!
WHAT'S GOING ON?
CHEER CHEER
◂chapter.24▸ end

MARS
TOKYOPOP®
A Bad Boy Can Change
A Good Girl Forever.
Graphic Novels On Sale
April 2002!
©Fuyumi Soryo. All Rights Reserved. TOKYOPOP is a registered trademark of Mixx Entertainment, Inc.
100% AUTHENTIC MANGA
品質第一公式商品

INITIAL 頭文字D
From Zero to Legend in 60 seconds...
100% AUTHENTIC MANGA
Gear up.
Initial D is coming.
Graphic Novels On Sale May 2002
Anime Coming Soon!
TOKYOPOP
"Initial D" First and Second Stage (24min x 39 episodes) © Shuichi Shigeno / KODANSHA / prime direction / OB PLANNING; "Initial D" Extra Stage (30min x 2 episodes) © Shuichi Shigeno / KODANSHA / to max / OB PLANNING. TOKYOPOP is a registered trademark of Mixx Entertainment, Inc.

STOP!

This is the back of the book.
ou wouldn't want to spoil a great ending!

This book is printed "manga-style," in the authentic Japanese right-to-left format. Since none of the artwork has been flipped or altered, readers get to experience the story just as the creator intended. You've been asking for it, so TOKYOPOP® delivered: authentic, hot-off-the-press, and far more fun!

DIRECTIONS

If this is your first time reading manga-style, here's a quick guide to help you understand how it works.

It's easy... just start in the top right panel and follow the numbers. Have fun, and look for more 100% authentic manga from TOKYOPOP®!